# 'The Female Marine' in an Era of Good Feelings: Cross-Dressing and the 'Genius' of Nathaniel Coverly, Jr.

## DANIEL A. COHEN

SOME LITERARY WORKS achieve success through the gradual accretion of sales and editions over a period of many years; others win a more fleeting notoriety, evoking intense interest within a relatively short span of time and then, almost as quickly, sinking into oblivion. The following essay examines a remarkable example of the latter category, a series of three linked narratives that briefly captivated New England readers in the immediate aftermath of the War of 1812. Eventually published together as a single volume entitled *The Female Marine*, the narratives recount the unlikely adventures of a young woman from rural Massachusetts who overcomes the stigma of a youthful seduction by first demonstrating military heroism and finally attaining a happy mar-

---

The first draft of this essay was written in 1986 during the American Antiquarian Society's Summer Seminar in the History of the Book in American Culture, led by the late Stephen Botein. A subsequent revision was delivered in July 1992, both as a Summer Lunchtime Colloquium at the American Antiquarian Society and at the fourteenth annual meeting of the Society for Historians of the Early American Republic in Gettysburg, Pennsylvania. I would like to thank the American Antiquarian Society for supporting my research on *The Female Marine* with a Stephen Botein Fellowship during the summer of 1992 and for providing the illustrations for this article. I am also grateful to Georgia B. Barnhill, Richard D. Brown, Sueann Caulfield, Morris L. Cohen, Patricia Cline Cohen, John Hench, Susan E. Klepp, Rosalind Remer, Caroline Sloat, Mary S. Zboray, Ronald J. Zboray, and the anonymous reviewers for their advice, assistance, and encouragement.

---

DANIEL A. COHEN, assistant professor of history at Florida International University, is the author of *Pillars of Salt, Monuments of Grace: New England Crime Literature and the Origins of American Popular Culture, 1674–1860* (1993). This essay is part of a book in progress, tentatively entitled *Beyond Domesticity: Documentary Images of Working-Class Women, 1815–1860*.

Copyright © 1994 by American Antiquarian Society

riage. Although no fewer than nineteen printings or editions of the various female-marine narratives were issued between 1815 and 1818, no more appeared until the publication of a modern scholarly edition in 1966.[1]

Like *The Female Marine* itself, this essay consists of three parts. The first part provides a basic description of the social context, publishing history, probable authorship, likely readership, and surprising plot of the female marine narratives. The second places the narratives in a somewhat broader literary context as 'epistemological texts' that manipulated the conventions of a number of popular formulaic genres without strictly conforming to any one of them. By selectively adopting—and adapting—the conventions of Female Warrior ballads and narratives, urban exposés, and sentimental seduction tales, the popular pamphlets constructed a vision of female autonomy and self-assertion far more radical than the images of Republican Wife, Republican Mother, and True Woman widely celebrated in the early republic.[2] The third part argues that the striking modernity of *The Female Marine*—particularly its image of unconventional womanhood—was rooted not only in the optimism and patriotism of the Era of Good Feelings but also in feelings of anxiety over the growth of urban vice in Boston and guilt over New England's notorious disloyalty during the war with England. Most broadly, this essay is a case study of the intricate interconnections between authorial creativity, literary formulae, and collective experience in the making of an ephemeral bestseller.

1. For basic bibliographic information on the various separate and composite nineteenth-century editions of the female-marine narratives, see Appendix A. For the twentieth-century edition, see Alexander Medlicott, Jr., ed., *The Female Marine or Adventures of Miss Lucy Brewer* (New York: Da Capo Press, 1966).
2. For scholarly discussions of those popular images, see Jan Lewis, 'The Republican Wife: Virtue and Seduction in the Early Republic,' *William and Mary Quarterly*, 3rd ser., 44 (October 1987): 689–721; Linda K. Kerber, *Women of the Republic: Intellect and Ideology in Revolutionary America* (Chapel Hill: University of North Carolina Press, 1980), pp. 283–88 and passim; Mary Beth Norton, *Liberty's Daughters: The Revolutionary Experience of American Women, 1750–1800* (Boston: Little, Brown and Company, 1980), pp. 242–50 and passim; Barbara Welter, 'The Cult of True Womanhood: 1820–1860,' *American Quarterly* 18 (Summer 1966): 151–74. Also see Ruth H. Bloch, 'The Gendered Meanings of Virtue in Revolutionary America,' *Signs* 13 (Autumn 1987): 37–58.

## I

Our textbooks assure us that the War of 1812 was an extremely unpopular conflict throughout much of New England, especially in Federalist port towns like Boston.[3] For years, merchants of the region had seen more economic harm in Republican embargoes than in British impressments, and many New Englanders greeted Congress's preparations for combat with alarm. In late April 1812, less than two months before the official declaration of war, no fewer than 455 Boston merchants frantically petitioned Congress for a postponement of hostilities.[4] Their warnings seemed to be vindicated by the generally disastrous course of the conflict that ensued, as American defeat followed defeat, climaxed by the burning of the nation's capital. Yet Boston's entrepreneurs seem to have been more upset by their own economic woes. By the autumn of 1813, there were 250 ships sitting idle in Boston harbor and people were leaving the city in search of employment.[5] 'We are in a deplorable situation,' a Massachusetts Federalist lamented in October 1814, 'our commerce dead; our revenue gone; our ships rotting at the wharves. . . . Our treasury drained—we are bankrupts.'[6] The following December and January, with the situation looking grim, representatives of the New England states met at Hartford in an ill-timed expression of regional dismay over government policies. But when news of a peace treaty and of Jackson's great victory in New Orleans reached them in February 1815, even disgruntled New Englanders responded with relief and jubilation.[7]

Still, Bostonians could not rest entirely easy while their beloved

---

3. See, for example, Thomas A. Bailey and David M. Kennedy, *The American Pageant*, 9th ed. 2 vols. (Lexington, Mass.: D. C. Heath, 1991), I: 212–20; Donald R. Hickey, *The War of 1812: A Forgotten Conflict* (Urbana: University of Illinois Press, 1989), pp. 255–80. On Boston as a Federalist town, note that the Federalist candidate for governor never received less than sixty-two percent of the Boston vote in any election between 1811 and 1818; see *Columbian Centinel*, April 3, 1811, p. 2; April 8, 1812, p. 2; April 7, 1813, p. 2; April 6, 1814, p. 2; April 5, 1815, p. 2; April 3, 1816, p. 2; April 9, 1817, p. 2; April 8, 1818, p. 2.
4. Roger H. Brown, *The Republic in Peril: 1812* (1964; reprint, New York: W. W. Norton, 1971), p. 104.
5. Hickey, *The War of 1812*, p. 231.
6. Quoted in Hickey, ibid.
7. For evidence of the relief and jubilation with which Bostonians received news of the end of the war, see *Columbian Centinel*, February 25, 1815, pp. 1–2; March 8, 1815, p. 1.

*Constitution* remained in danger—not the document, about which many of them felt somewhat ambivalent, but the ship, which remained subject to British attack despite the peace. Affectionately dubbed Old Ironsides, the frigate *Constitution*, built and based in Boston, had achieved one of the first American naval victories of the war in August 1812 and thereafter became a potent symbol of national military prowess much celebrated in popular ballads.[8] Even New Englanders who ardently opposed the war—and suffered its deprivations—expressed patriotic pride in the *Constitution*'s triumphs.[9] 'No nation ever possessed a vessel which had more . . . deserved popularity,' the editor of Boston's leading Federalist newspaper declared in mid-April 1815, 'and the solicitude for her safety is general, affectionate and profound.'[10] While the war was officially over by then, hostilities persisted at sea, and Boston newspaper readers anxiously followed a series of updates on the status of the *Constitution*. On April 19, for example, the *Columbian Centinel* cited a report that the American vessel had been captured; a week later it happily reported that Old Ironsides had successfully evaded a British squadron.[11] When the *Constitution* finally arrived safely in Boston harbor at the end of May, the inhabitants of the town responded with exuberance. As the ship cast anchor and its officers disembarked, flags waved, artillery roared, and a band played patriotic tunes. Crowds of citizens of both sexes filled the streets, wharves, vessels, and house windows, adding to the general commotion with their hearty cheers and shouts. It may have been a bad war but it certainly was an exhilarating peace—after all, the *Constitution* had come through with colors flying.[12]

8. See Tyrone G. Martin, *A Most Fortunate Ship: A Narrative History of 'Old Ironsides'* (Chester, Conn.: Globe Pequot Press, 1980), pp. 124–25, 168.
9. See Benjamin W. Labaree, *Patriots and Partisans: The Merchants of Newburyport, 1764–1815*. (1962; reprint, New York: W. W. Norton, 1975), pp. 187, 191.
10. *Columbian Centinel*, April 12, 1815, p. 2.
11. *Columbian Centinel*, April 12, 1815, p. 2; April 15, 1815, p. 2; April 19, 1815, p. 2; April 22, 1815, p. 2; April 26, 1815, p. 2; *Daily Advertiser*, April 12, 1815, p. 2; *Yankee*, April 14, 1815, p. 2; May 12, 1815, p. 2.
12. *Daily Advertiser*, May 30, 1815, p. 2; *Columbian Centinel*, May 31, 1815, pp. 2–3; *Independent Chronicle*, June 1, 1815, p. 2. On the limited participation of American women

One canny Boston entrepreneur named Nathaniel Coverly, Jr., saw the happy conclusion of the war and the triumphant return of the *Constitution* as occasions not only for patriotism but also for profit. The son of an itinerant printer, publisher, and bookseller, Coverly followed in the footsteps of his enterprising father, earning a precarious livelihood in Boston by printing cheap pamphlets and broadsides for common readers, often on criminal or military themes.[13] The younger Coverly is probably best remembered today as the printer of almost all of the 300 or so broadside ballads purchased by the great American printer Isaiah Thomas in 1814 and donated by him to the American Antiquarian Society as a permanent record of popular—or, as he put it, 'vulgar'—taste.[14] Many of those ballads related to American victories in the then-ongoing war with England, and several dealt specifically with the famous naval victories of Old Ironsides.[15] Even in Federalist Boston there seems to have been a ready market for such works. After all, close to one third of the inhabitants voted for Republican candidates throughout the war and, as noted above, even those who did not support the Republican war effort took pride in the martial exploits of American (particularly local) ships and sailors. According to one source, Boston sailors were themselves among Coverly's chief patrons.[16] By 1815 Coverly was no novice at cash-

---

in public celebrations during the nineteenth century, see Mary P. Ryan, *Women in Public: Between Banners and Ballots, 1825–1880* (Baltimore: Johns Hopkins University Press, 1990), pp. 19–57.

13. For general information on both Coverlys, see Benjamin Franklin V, ed., *Boston Printers, Publishers, and Booksellers: 1640–1800* (Boston: G. K. Hall, 1980), pp. 76–81. On the precariousness of their livelihood, see the American Antiquarian Society's printers file which cites newspaper notices indicating that both of the Coverlys had a brush with bankruptcy in 1802; for the actual notices, see *Independent Chronicle*, November 15, 1802; December 20, 1802.

14. See Worthington C. Ford, *The Isaiah Thomas Collection of Ballads* (Worcester, Mass.: American Antiquarian Society, 1924), pp. 19–22 and passim; also see Arthur F. Schrader, 'Broadside Ballads of Boston, 1813: The Isaiah Thomas Collection,' *Proceedings of the American Antiquarian Society* 98 (April 1988): 69–111.

15. Ibid., pp. 6–11 and passim.

16. The Republican vote for governor in Boston between 1812 and 1815 fluctuated between twenty-nine and thirty-two percent; see citations for the appropriate years from the *Columbian Centinel* in note 3. For a discussion of several patriotic cartoons issued in New England during the War of 1812, see Georgia Brady Barnhill, 'Political Cartoons of New England, 1812–61,' in Georgia B. Barnhill, ed., *Prints of New England* (Worcester:

ing in on the patriotism of such readers; yet he knew how to appeal to their prurient interests as well.[17] In the aftermath of the *Constitution's* triumphant return to Boston, Coverly came up with a formula that would appeal to both.

In mid-August 1815, Coverly inserted notices in two of Boston's Republican newspapers advertising a pamphlet entitled *An Affecting Narrative of Louisa Baker*.[18] The title page of the first edition indicated that it had been printed in New York by one Luther Wales. However, that imprint was almost certainly a fiction contrived by Coverly, perhaps as a 'cover' in the event that Boston authorities were offended by the racy work.[19] For the narrative was typical of Coverly's output—and his name appeared proudly on three subsequent editions. A few months later, in November 1815, Coverly advertised a sequel to the Baker narrative entitled *The Adventures of Lucy Brewer*, followed in May 1816 by a third installment of the series, entitled *An Awful Beacon to the Rising Generation*.[20] Several composite editions of the narratives appeared throughout 1816 and thereafter under the title of *The Female Marine*. In all, copies survive of at least nineteen printings or editions of *The Female Marine* and its shorter components, all

---

American Antiquarian Society, 1991), pp. 86–88. On Boston sailors as a prime market for the Coverlys' ephemeral productions, see the unidentified newspaper clipping, ca. 1866–82, inserted between pages 34 and 35 of Melvin Lord, 'Boston Booksellers, 1650–1860,' Boston Booksellers Papers 1640–1860, American Antiquarian Society [cited hereafter as Unidentified Newspaper Clipping]. I am very grateful to Ronald and Mary Zboray for bringing that newspaper clipping to my attention.

17. For discussion of an example of Coverly's appeal to prurient interests, see Daniel A. Cohen, *Pillars of Salt, Monuments of Grace: New England Crime Literature and the Origins of American Popular Culture 1674–1860*, (New York: Oxford University Press, 1993), pp. 178–82.

18. See *Boston Patriot*, August 16, 1815, p. 3; *The Yankee*, August 18, 1815, p. 3.

19. I have found no evidence that 'Luther Wales' ever published any other books or pamphlets, and New York City directories of the years from 1813 through 1817 do not list anyone by that name; see the various editions of *Longworth's American Almanac, New-York Register, and City Directory* (New York: David Longworth) for the years 1813 through 1817; also *The Citizens Directory and Strangers Guide* (New York: George Long, 1814). No other publications by 'Luther Wales' appear in the American Antiquarian Society's extensive printers file or in the relevant index to Shaw and Shoemaker; see Frances P. Newton, comp., *American Bibliography: A Preliminary Checklist, 1801 to 1819 . . . Printers, Publishers and Booksellers Index* (Metuchen, N.J.: Scarecrow Press, 1983), p. 317. My conclusion is that 'Luther Wales' was a pseudonym concocted by Nathaniel Coverly, Jr.

20. *The Yankee*, November 17, 1815, p. 3; May 3, 1816, p. 3.

produced between 1815 and 1818. (See Appendix A.) For a period of a few years, they must have been among the most widely circulated pamphlets in Boston.

Although many of them list no printer or publisher on their title pages, most of the female-marine pamphlets were almost certainly issued by Nathaniel Coverly, Jr. While it is possible that he wrote the narratives himself, it seems more likely that they were compiled by a hack author in his employ. Indeed, according to an unidentified newspaper clipping in the collections of the American Antiquarian Society, Coverly 'kept a poet, or ready writer, who manufactured for him all prose and verse articles which were called for by the occasions of the time.' The clipping described that author—appropriately named 'Mr. Wright'—as 'a comical genius, who could do the grave or the gay, as necessity demanded, and with equal facility.' Such a good-humored and versatile 'genius' would have been just the sort to have concocted the playful and eclectic story of the female marine.[21]

The author referred to in the newspaper clipping was probably Nathaniel Hill Wright, an obscure printer, publisher, editor, and poet who produced several works in verse under his own name during the early decades of the nineteenth century.[22] Wright first appeared on the literary scene in 1808, at about the age of twenty-one, when he penned a broadside Fourth of July *Ode* addressed to 'Republican young men.'[23] He married the following year in Boston and his wife gave birth to a boy in Newburyport just six months later.[24] Several years after that, apparently while living in Vermont,

21. Unidentified Newspaper Clipping. It should also be noted that the *The Awful Beacon* includes a copyright notice in Coverly's name, which suggests that it was likely written either by him or by someone in his employ.

22. For basic information and sources on Wright, see the American Antiquarian Society printers file and printers authority cards. He is listed as a "printer" in a number of Boston city directories; see *The Boston Directory* (Boston: E. Cotton, 1813), p. 270; *The Boston Directory* (Boston: E. Cotton, 1818), p. 231; *The Boston Directory* (Boston: John H. A. Frost and Charlest Stimpson, Jr., 1820), p. 226; *The Boston Directory* (John H. A. Frost and Charles Stimpson, Jr., 1821), p. 259; *The Boston Directory* (Boston: John H. A. Frost and Charles Stimpson, Jr., 1822), p. 256.

23. Nathaniel H. Wright, *Ode, Written for the Celebrarion* [sic] *of the Republican Young Men, July 4, 1808* ([Boston?]: [1808]).

24. For the approximate date of Wright's marriage, see *Columbian Centinel*, November

Fig. 1. Patriotic front cover of *The Female Marine* ([Boston?]: [N. Coverly, Jr.?], June 19, 1816), with a cut of the Great Seal of the United States. Courtesy, American Antiquarian Society.

he produced two small volumes of poetry that featured patriotic verses on American naval exploits in the War of 1812, including a couple of pieces relating to the frigate *Constitution*.[25] Back in Massachusetts in 1819, he composed a pamphlet entitled *Boston: or A Touch at the Times*, a poetical tour of the city that was alternately 'descriptive, serious, and satirical.' Toward the end of the pamphlet, in some verses that are surely autobiographical, Wright describes a dejected poet who feels obliged to abandon his higher literary aspirations in order to churn out 'doleful ditties, murders, and the like' that will appeal to the 'wondering multitude.'[26] At the time of the first appearance of *The Female Marine*, Wright was in his late twenties, a family man with a wife and at least one small child, evidently struggling to make ends meet.[27] While none of this *proves* that Nathaniel Hill Wright was the author of the female-marine narratives, his political affiliation, sexual history, literary predilections, self characterization, and personal circumstances—along with the newspaper reference identifying 'Mr. Wright' as Coverly's hack—all tend to make him a very plausible candidate.

According to the Antiquarian Society's helpful clipping, the main customers for Coverly's broadsides were 'sailors,' 'the Ann street population of that day' (i.e. prostitutes and their compa-

---

18, 1809, p. 2; however, also see *A Volume of Records Relating to the Early History of Boston, Containing Boston Marriages, From 1752 to 1809* (Boston: Municipal Printing Office, 1903), p. 387, which places the marriage nearly a month earlier. For the approximate birthdate of his son (May 27, 1810), see *Vital Records of Newburyport, Massachusetts to the End of the Year 1849*, 2 vols. (Salem, Mass.: Essex Institute, 1911), I: 424.

25. Nathaniel H. Wright, *Monody, On the Death of Brigadier General Zebulon Montgomery Pike, and Other Poems* (Middlebury, (Vt.): Slade & Ferguson, 1814), pp. 25–36; Nathaniel H. Wright, *The Fall of Palmyra: and Other Poems* (Middlebury, (Vt.): William Slade, Jun., 1817), pp. 99–108. That Wright, according to the prefaces to those works, seems to have been living in Middlebury, Vermont, in June 1814 and again in December 1816 does present a bit of a problem in trying to link him to Coverly and *The Female Marine*; however, those stays may have been brief or intermittent, and it is clear (from the directories cited in note 22 and other evidence in the AAS printers file) that he was living in Boston in 1813 and was back there by 1818 at the latest.

26. See Nathaniel H. Wright, *Boston: or A Touch At the Times* (Boston: Hews & Goss, 1819), t.p. and 19–20.

27. See ibid., pp. 19–20. For Wright's approximate age, see his obituary; *Columbian Centinel*, May 15, 1824, p. 2. For references to his wife and child, see note 24.

triots), and 'juveniles.'[28] Coverly probably intended a similar readership for the female marine narratives, though in this case he seems to have particularly targeted the 'juveniles.' A note on the title page of the third part pronounces it 'worthy the perusal of young persons of both sexes, and of all classes.'[29] With the first and second parts priced at a very modest twelve and a half cents each—roughly equivalent to the cost of a mass-market paperback to an unskilled laborer in the late twentieth century—the pamphlets would have been accessible to all but the most impoverished of readers.[30] It may be significant that at least three out of the four early owners' signatures on surviving copies are those of women, probably young women. One of them neatly noted inside the front cover—underlining for emphasis—that *The Female Marine* was 'a very interesting Book Indeed.'[31] Other readers seem to have agreed; about half of the known editions survive only in a single copy—typically worn and tattered—suggesting that many of the modest volumes were literally read to pieces by their eager purchasers.[32]

And no wonder, as a quick plot summary will make clear. Part

---

28. Unidentified Newspaper Clipping. On Ann Street as a notorious neighborhood for prostitutes, see Barbara Meil Hobson, *Uneasy Virtue: The Politics of Prostitution and the American Reform Tradition* (New York: Basic Books, 1987), p. 26.

29. *The Awful Beacon* (Boston: N. Coverly, Jr., 1816), t.p.

30. On the prices of parts one and two, see *The Yankee*, August 18, 1815, p. 3; November 17, 1815, p. 3. According to the Massachusetts Bureau of Statistics of Labor, a 'medium' daily wage for a Massachusetts laborer was $.987 in 1815 and $1.07 in 1816; see Carroll D. Wright, *History of Wages and Prices in Massachusetts: 1752-1883* (Boston: Wright & Potter, 1885), pp. 82 and 84. The cost of a twelve-and-a-half-cent pamphlet for such a laborer would thus be approximately twelve percent of his daily wage; that would be almost identical (as a percentage of daily wages) to the cost of a $4.95 mass market paperback to an unskilled laborer working an eight-hour day at about $5.00 an hour in 1994. Obviously, that is a somewhat crude measure of affordability, given possible fluctuations in the relative costs of food, lodging, and other necessities.

31. See owners' signatures on American Antiquarian Society copies of *The Adventures of Louisa Baker* (New York: Luther Wales, [1815]); *The Female Marine, or Adventures of Miss Lucy Brewer* ([Boston?]: [N. Coverly, Jr.?], May 30, 1816); *The Female Marine, or Adventures of Miss Lucy Brewer*, 2nd ed., ([Boston?]: [N. Coverly, Jr.?], June 19, 1816); *The Female Marine, or Adventures of Miss Lucy Brewer* (Hartwick, N.Y.: L. & B. Todd, [1816?]), from which the inscription is quoted.

32. For locations of most surviving copies of the various editions, see Shaw and Shoemaker citations in Appendix A. The majority of located copies are at the American Antiquarian Society.

one describes the adventures of Louisa Baker, a teenage girl from rural Massachusetts, who is seduced by an insincere lover. The fallen and pregnant young woman soon moves to Boston, where she finds shelter in a brothel and gives birth to a baby. After the infant dies, Louisa is coerced into prostitution, a vocation that she follows for three years. At that point, in 1812 or 1813, she disguises herself as a man, escapes from her brothel, and enlists as a United States marine.[33] She serves bravely on board the *Constitution* for two or three years and, in 1815, reassumes her female identity, returning as 'a true penitent' to her parents.[34]

In part two, the young veteran, now identified as Lucy Brewer (alias Louisa Baker), becomes restless living at home with her parents and decides to travel. She again disguises herself as a man and boards a stagecoach heading southward on which a fellow passenger, a wealthy young woman from New York named Miss West, is abused by an impertinent midshipman. Lucy intervenes and rescues the girl by accepting the sailor's challenge to a duel. Thoroughly intimidating the young man with a clever bluff, Lucy avoids any actual bloodshed. Lucy then travels to New York, where she spends some time with Miss West and her brother. Returning to Boston still dressed as a man, Lucy visits her old brothel and some former shipmates before returning to her parents.[35]

In part three, Mr. West, the brother of the girl whom Lucy had rescued on the stage coach, discovers that the good samaritan was, in fact, a woman and travels up to Massachusetts to court her. The two visit Plymouth Rock, where Mr. West launches into a patriotic disquisition on the Pilgrims. Later West proposes to Lucy; she accepts; her father agrees to the match—one imagines with a good

---

33. There is an internal contradiction in the narratives concerning the timing of Baker's enlistment; although the pamphlets indicate that she enlisted in 1813, they describe her participation in battles that actually took place in 1812.

34. This paragraph summarizes *Adventures of Louisa Baker*, or *The Female Marine, or the Adventures of Miss Lucy Brewer*, 10th ed., ([Boston?]: Printed for the Proprietor [N. Coverly, Jr.?], 1816), pp. [7]–51. The 'tenth' is the most complete of the composite editions; all subsequent citations of *The Female Marine* will be to that edition unless otherwise indicated.

35. This paragraph summarizes *The Adventures of Lucy Brewer* (Boston: N. Coverly, Jr., 1815), or *Female Marine*, pp. [53]–92.

deal of relief—and the former Boston prostitute is happily married to the wealthy New Yorker. In addition to the main plot line, parts two and three of the narrative also include some supplementary warnings and moral sketches, further illustrating the destructive consequences of sexual vice.[36]

The first narrative of the female marine and its two sequels were so popular with New England readers that Coverly produced at least two additional spinoffs. In late June 1816, Coverly advertised a pamphlet entitled *A Brief Reply to the Late Writings of Louisa Baker* by Mrs. Rachel Sperry. The ostensible author, identified as the madam of the brothel in which Baker claimed to have been entrapped, revealed that Baker's real name was Eliza Bowen and indignantly denied that Bowen had been an unwilling participant in prostitution. Sperry also defended her own involvement in the sex trade as a necessary recourse, following the sudden death of her husband, to save her family from 'misery and want.'[37] In early September 1816, Coverly advertised another pamphlet entitled *The Surprising Adventures of Almira Paul*. This new heroine had an even more varied and unlikely career than 'the female marine,' serving in male disguise on board English, American, and Algerine naval vessels before marrying an English war widow in Portsmouth, England. Paul was determined to 'convince the world that the capacities of *women* were equal to that of the *men*' but was, the story went, eventually forced to abandon her disguise and work in the vice districts of Baltimore, New York, and Boston as a prostitute.[38] It was not until late October 1816 that Coverly finally beat a strategic retreat from the daring themes of female sexuality, autonomy, and adventure, advertising *A Brief Account of the Happy*

36. This paragraph summarizes *The Awful Beacon, to the Rising Generation of Both Sexes* (Boston: N. Coverly, Jr., 1816), or *Female Marine*, pp. [97]–142. For the supplementary warnings and moral sketches, see *Female Marine*, pp. 81–92 and [131]–42.

37. *The Yankee*, June 21, 1816, p. 3; Rachel Sperry, *A Brief Reply to the Late Writings of Louisa Baker* (Boston: M. Brewster, 1816) quoted on p. 5. This pamphlet was probably concocted by Nathaniel Coverly in order to enhance the verisimilitude of the earlier female-marine pamphlets; the imprint 'M. Brewster' may be yet another pseudonym for Coverly.

38. *The Yankee*, September 6, 1816, p. 3; *The Surprising Adventures of Almira Paul* (Boston: N. Coverly, Jr., 1816), passim, quoted on p. 13. This work is probably fictional.

*Death of Mary Ann Clark*, the narrative of a much more conventional heroine. Perhaps as an antidote to its immediate predecessors, the story of Miss Clark was designed to provide 'an example of meekness and submission,' along with 'the clearest evidence of early Piety.'[39]

## II

Although all editions of *The Female Marine* and its component parts are presented as factual accounts—and have been taken as such by uncritical readers ever since—they are almost certainly works of fiction.[40] Such, at least, was the considered judgment of the first academic historian to study the narratives, Alexander Medlicott, Jr. He systematically checked the vital records of all twenty-six towns in early national Plymouth County, the putative site of the female marine's birth, and found no evidence whatsoever of the existence of any Louisa Baker, Lucy Brewer, Lucy West, or Eliza Bowen, as the female marine is variously designated in Coverly's several pamphlets. He also checked the muster rolls of the frigate *Constitution* and found no marine aboard the ship with the first or last name of George, the moniker under which the female marine supposedly served.[41] More recently, I have undertaken similar investigations of the elusive marine with no more success than Medlicott.

Even if one accepts its general designation as fiction—and it would have been difficult for contemporary readers to be sure—*The Female Marine* is far from being a simple work to categorize. 'Like most novels of the early nineteenth century in America it is a composite,' Medlicott explains, 'a blend of many types of popular contemporary styles, themes, and techniques: romance, memoir,

---

39. *The Yankee*, October 25, 1816, p. 3. The Clark narrative is an example of a long Anglo-American tradition of accounts of the pious conversions and deaths of children that originated during the seventeenth century with James Janeway's *A Token for Children*.

40. For an example of a twentieth-century author who seems to believe in the reality of Lucy Brewer, see Edward Rowe Snow, *Unsolved Mysteries of Sea and Shore* (London: Alvin Redman, 1964), pp. 111–13.

41. See Alexander Medlicott, Jr., 'The Legend of Lucy Brewer: An Early American Novel,' *New England Quarterly* 39 (1966): 465–67; Medlicott, ed., *The Female Marine*, pp. xvii–xxiii.

pseudo-history, adventure, picaresque tale, autobiography, and sermon.'[42] The ambiguity in generic identity is paralleled by the multiple uncertainties and misperceptions experienced by characters within the plot itself. Male or female, vice or virtue, bravery or cowardice, happiness or sorrow, youth or old age, dream or reality—all of those conventional—and conventionally self-evident—polarities are confused or blurred at one point or another by various characters within the narrative.[43]

That sort of problematizing of perception both for actors within the plot and for 'external' readers is characteristic of a type of complex narrative identified by literary scholar Thomas Kent as 'epistemological texts.' In such texts, Kent explains, 'epistemological uncertainty may be seen to function on two levels: on the narrative level within the text where characters and events are interwoven, and on the extra-textual level, or audience level, where judgments must be made by the reader about the meaning of the text.'[44] In the case of *The Female Marine*, even that most basic distinction between text and audience is subverted when characters in the third part of the narrative are influenced by their own reading of the first installment; thus the fragmented text itself becomes an active agent within the plot—serving, ironically, to correct a key misperception by two of its characters. Kent contrasts complex 'epistemological texts' to the relatively simple and highly formulaic dime novels of the late nineteenth century which he describes as 'automatized texts.'[45] Part of the epistemological havoc generated by *The Female Marine* is caused by its selective appropriation of motifs from a number of popular formulaic genres—or 'automatized texts'—familiar to early-nineteenth-century readers.[46]

42. Medlicott, 'The Legend of Lucy Brewer,' p. 471.
43. The confusion over sexual identity pervades the text. On the confusion between vice and virtue, see *Female Marine*, pp. 7–9 and 21–26; between bravery and cowardice, pp. 58–65; between youth and old age, see pp. 85–86 and 88; between dream and reality, p. 124; between happiness and sorrow, pp. 127–28.
44. See Thomas Kent, *Interpretation and Genre: The Role of Generic Perception in the Study of Narrative Texts* (Lewisburg, Pa.: Bucknell University Press, 1986), pp. 124–42 quoted on p. 126.
45. Kent, *Interpretation and Genre*, 81–101.
46. To describe Female Warrior ballads and narratives, urban exposés, and sentimental

# The Female Marine

First, Coverly's pamphlets are part of a long tradition of Female Warrior ballads and narratives in early modern popular literature.[47] In her recent monograph *Warrior Women and Popular Balladry*, literary scholar Dianne Dugaw locates no fewer than 120 different Anglo-American Female Warrior ballads printed mostly in Great Britain between the seventeenth and nineteenth centuries, along with many prose narratives on the same theme. Indeed, she claims that 'the Female Warrior and masquerading heroines like her were an imaginative preoccupation of the early modern era, appearing not only in popular street ballads but in a host of other genres as well: epic, romance, biography, comedy, tragedy, opera, and ballad opera.' According to Dugaw, the early modern tradition of Female Warriors emerged at the dawn of the seventeenth century, reached the height of its vogue during the eighteenth century, and declined in popularity during the early nineteenth century.[48] At least a few of the Female Warrior ballads identified by Dugaw seem to have been printed and sold by the Coverlys of early national Boston.[49] In addition, American *prose* narratives of cross-dressing female soldiers were published in connection with the Revolution, the War of 1812, the Mexican War, and the Civil War.[50] The first of those accounts—the narrative of

---

seduction tales as 'formulaic genres' does not preclude the possibility—even likelihood—that individual examples would contain creative, idiosyncratic, and unconventional elements. *The Female Marine* is an extreme case in point. For that reason, I am uncomfortable with the designation 'automatized texts.'

47. See Dianne Dugaw, *Warrior Women and Popular Balladry, 1650–1850* (Cambridge: Cambridge University Press, 1989); Julie Wheelwright, *Amazons and Military Maids: Women Who Dressed as Men in the Pursuit of Life, Liberty and Happiness* (London: Pandora, 1989); Simon Shepherd, *Amazons and Warrior Women: Varieties of Feminism in Seventeenth-Century Drama* (New York: St. Martin's Press, 1981). On the same phenomenon in early-modern Holland, see Rudolph M. Dekker and Lotte C. van de Pol, *The Tradition of Female Transvestism in Early Modern Europe* (New York: St. Martin's Press, 1989).

48. See Dugaw, *Warrior Women*, pp. 1–3, 10, and passim.

49. See *Female Drummer*; *The Happy Ship Carpenter*; *A Lover's Lamentation for the Girl He Left Behind Him; and Her Answer*, all in the Isaiah Thomas ballad collection at the American Antiquarian Society in Worcester; also listed in Ford, *Isaiah Thomas Collection*, nos. 87, 112, 155–56, and 253. Also see Dugaw, *Warrior Women*, p. 87.

50. Aside from the female-marine series on the War of 1812, see, for example, Herman Mann, *The Female Review: Life of Deborah Sampson, the Female Soldier of the War of the Revolution*, ed. John Adams Vinton (1866; reprint, New York: Arno Press, 1972); Ned Buntline [Edward Judson], *The Volunteer; or, The Maid of Monterey* (Boston: F. Gleason, 1847); *The Woman in Battle: A Narrative of the Exploits, Adventures, and Travels of Madame*

a Revolutionary war veteran named Deborah Sampson Gannett (alias Robert Shurtleff)—is repeatedly cited by the heroine of *The Female Marine*, both as the inspiration for her own exploits and as a documented precedent to bolster the credibility of her tale.[51]

Modern scholars, particularly feminist scholars, have been fascinated by the gender politics embedded in Female Warrior ballads and narratives. Cross-dressing women certainly destabilize the culturally constructed distinction between male and female. However, one might argue that Female Warrior ballads do so in a way that privileges masculine virtue; after all, Female Warriors are celebrated—and they invariably *are* celebrated in the popular literature—for their adoption of conventionally male behaviors.[52] In addition, Female Warriors in the early modern literature are generally motivated by a traditional feminine goal: their desire to be reunited with husbands or lovers gone off to war. Thus Dugaw explains that 'almost all' of the ballads and 'most' of the prose narratives 'make [heterosexual] love the heroine's ultimate motive.'[53] By contrast, Louisa Baker goes to war not to 'stand by her man' but rather to escape her entrapment within an exploitative system of commercialized sex. Her conventional marriage at the end of the narrative is not presented as the motive for her exploits but rather as a reward for her aggressive pursuit of autonomy and personal fulfillment. In that regard, at least, *The Female Marine* is distinctly more radical than most earlier Female Warrior narratives.

Coverly's pamphlets also stand near the beginning of what became a prolific nineteenth-century tradition of urban exposés.

---

*Loreta Janeta Velazquez, Otherwise Known as Lieutenant Harry T. Buford, Confederate States Army*, ed. C. J. Worthington (Hartford: T. Belknap, 1876).

51. See Mann, *Female Review*; *Female Marine*, pp. 36, 49, and 55–56. The real-life case of Gannett, who actually received a pension from the federal government, reminds us that the female warrior is not simply a literary tradition but a social tradition as well.

52. See Dugaw, *Warrior Women*, pp. 143–62. See especially on pp. 158–59 where Dugaw rejects that conservative reading of the ballads: 'the ballads do not in fact privilege the "masculine" at all, because at a deeper level they actually subvert not only the privilege of one gender over the other, but the very category of gender itself.'

53. See Dugaw, *Warrior Women*, pp. 35, 92–93, 113, 130, and 131.

According to Lyle Wright, only two out of sixty-nine novels of 'city life' published in the United States between 1800 and 1850 appeared before 1820.[54] According to Adrienne Siegel's more comprehensive count, only eighteen 'urban novels' appeared in America during the period between 1774 and 1830, in contrast to the hundreds that poured from American presses during the 1840s and 1850s. Having thoroughly canvassed that vast output, Siegel suggests that mass-market urban fiction of the mid-nineteenth century conveyed an ambivalent vision of urban America. Many of the novels exposed the material hardships, social inequities, and moral dangers of city life. But at the same time, they tended to reinforce the claims of urban boosters that American cities were great repositories of cultural abundance and social opportunity.[55]

Coverly's female marine conveys a similarly split image of early national Boston. On the one hand, Lucy Brewer's portrait of Boston's seamy red-light district on 'Negro Hill' is extremely graphic. Her unromanticized descriptions of dance halls, brothels, seductive call girls, coarse street walkers, child prostitutes, and interracial sexual encounters surely shocked early-nineteenth-century readers.[56] At one point, Lucy suggests that Boston may have a 'greater proportion' of whores than 'any town of equal size in the Union.'[57] Judging from her lurid narrative, that is easy to believe. As an urban exposé with vivid descriptions that allow readers to indulge vicariously in that which they presumably deplore, *The Female Marine* is an early precursor to what David Reynolds has described as a vast antebellum literature of 'immoral didacticism' or 'subversive reform.'[58]

But on the other hand—and in Coverly's multivalent narrative there almost always is an other hand—several descriptions of Bos-

---

54. Lyle H. Wright, 'A Statistical Survey of American Fiction,' *Huntington Library Quarterly* 2 (April 1939): 314.
55. See Adrienne Siegel, *The Image of the American City in Popular Literature, 1820–1870* (Port Washington, N.Y.: Kennikat Press, 1981), p. 6 and passim.
56. *The Female Marine*, pp. 21–34 and 73–91, passim.
57. *Female Marine*, p. 132.
58. See David S. Reynolds, *Beneath the American Renaissance: The Subversive Imagination in the Age of Emerson and Melville* (New York: Alfred A. Knopf, 1988).

ton in *The Female Marine* make it read more like an advertisement than an exposé. In part one of the narrative, an informed observer claims of Boston that 'there is not a city or town in any part of the United States, that can boast of a greater proportion of honest, kind and hospitable inhabitants.'[59] Much later, in part three, Mr. West describes the 'capital of New-England' in similarly laudatory terms; Lucy's future husband

> ... represented the town, for pleasantness, &c. far surpassing his expectations, while upon its inhabitants, for their natural good humour and polite attention to strangers, he bestowed the highest encomiums. ... the many excellent bridges which connect the neighbouring villages with the town, for convenience and beauty of structure, he represented as far surpassing any that he had ever before seen—the State-House, for beauty, &c. he thought equal, and far more pleasantly situated than the City Hall of New-York, nor did he conceive the Bowery of that city half so pleasant as the justly admired Mall of Boston. . . . .[60]

Not only do Coverly's pamphlets anticipate both the muckraking and the boosterism of antebellum city novels, one of them even reconciles those two seemingly incompatible stances toward urban life. In her *Brief Reply* to Louisa Baker, Rachel Sperry claims that vice districts like Negro Hill actually purify the civic environment by segregating disreputable elements:

> ... that the existence of such places are [*sic*] essential to the security of the innocent and defenceless, in large commercial towns and cities, I have no doubt. What would be the situation of Boston, and what the danger attending the evening excursions of its female inhabitants, were not a peculiar class of their fellow-creatures priviledged [*sic*] with a place of resort like the Hill?—should those of easy life, peculiar to sea ports, be denied residence here, they would privately seek one in more respectable parts of the town—then would every female, however innocent and respectable, be liable to be insulted in their houses, and venture abroad in the evening at the risk of their lives. . . . sailors, soldiers, &c. who now uniformly resort to the hill, would then parole [*sic*] the public streets in search of company, and to whose insults and abuse every female, young and old, would be liable. Large towns and

59. *Female Marine*, p. 16.
60. *Female Marine*, pp. 117–18.

cities have found it always necessary to erect suitable places of deposit for all nuisances, filth, &c. whereby the health of its inhabitants are [sic] endangered—so for public good, in every large town and city, ought there to be a place allotted those who prefer a life of debauchery, and who are esteemed as a public nuisance—so far we consider the Hill, and its inhabitants . . . of public benefit to the town.[61]

By ignoring the coercion and exploitation that often pervade zones of urban vice—and by dehumanizing their principals—the author introduces a rationale for tolerating such districts that would be widely embraced by policymakers of the nineteenth and twentieth centuries, who often tried to contain or regulate prostitution rather than extirpate it.[62] However, it is probably significant that Coverly (or his hack) distances himself from that complacent position by attributing it to an author of dubious character. The more credible account of Louisa Baker—to which Sperry's narrative is opposed—features sharp and intolerant diatribes against the procurers, madams, and harlots of Negro Hill. As a group, Coverly's pamphlets thus present a multivalent vision of urban life—and of urban vice—that defies any simple formula.

Yet another conventional genre that *The Female Marine* impersonates, but transcends, is the sentimental seduction tale—the dominant form of early American fiction. Samuel Richardson's *Clarissa*, first published in England in 1748, provided an archetype for such early American novels as William Hill Brown's *The Power of Sympathy* (1789), Susanna Rowson's *Charlotte Temple* (1791), and Hannah Foster's *The Coquette* (1797). In all of those works, women are seduced by insincere lovers and then die (or commit suicide) out of shame or remorse.[63] Although seduction tales conveyed

---

61. Sperry, *Brief Reply*, pp. 14–15.
62. For perceptive historical studies of public policy toward prostitution in America and England respectively, see Barbara Meil Hobson, *Uneasy Virtue*, and Judith R. Walkowitz, *Prostitution and Victorian Society: Women, Class, and the State* (Cambridge: Cambridge University Press, 1980).
63. See Cathy N. Davidson, *Revolution and the Word: The Rise of the Novel in America* (New York: Oxford University Press, 1986), pp. 83–150; Leslie A. Fiedler, *Love and Death in the American Novel*, rev. ed. (1966; reprint, New York: Stein and Day, 1982), pp. 74–125 and passim; Herbert Ross Brown, *The Sentimental Novel in America, 1789–1860* (New York: Pageant Books, 1959), pp. 28–51; James D. Hart, *The Popular Book: A History of America's*

seemingly conservative messages of filial obedience and sexual restraint to their predominantly female readers, modern feminist scholars have argued that early seduction tales were actually a subversive genre that warned young women against male depravity, called for female solidarity, and assailed the sexual double standard.[64]

In some respects *The Female Marine*, particularly in its early pages, fits comfortably into the canon of early American sentimental fiction. As Alexander Medlicott observes, the author employs 'almost every device known to the writers of romance in the eighteenth century: parental warnings; headlong-heedless love; seduction by a dastardly villain; flight through storms; temporary sanctuary with a kindly protectress; ensnarement by a wretched deceiver; a pitiful death of an unwanted child; sermons and lectures on moral fiber; and years of depravity and disillusionment as a fallen woman.'[65] Most important, Lucy's seduction is remarkably similar to those depicted in the earlier novels. 'I was all innocence, and knew no sin, until that fatal period when the vile and insinuating author of my ruin deluded and deceived me,' Lucy recalls. 'I never once reflected that the man who could stoop to seduction, would not hesitate to forsake the wretched object of his passion.'[66] In short, the opening episodes of Coverly's narrative faithfully replicate the definitive motifs of the sentimental seduction tale.

*The Female Marine* also resembles other works of early American fiction in claiming a serious didactic purpose. Thus the narrator inserts a cautionary statement, typical of early sentimental novels,

---

*Literary Taste* (New York: Oxford University Press, 1950), pp. 51–57; Frank Luther Mott, *Golden Multitudes: The Story of Best Sellers in the United States* (New York: Macmillan, 1947), pp. 35–40.

64. See Davidson, *Revolution and the Word*, pp. 83–150, passim; for a somewhat similar analysis of a later body of sentimental fiction, see Jane Tompkins, *Sensational Designs: The Cultural Work of American Fiction, 1790–1860* (New York: Oxford University Press, 1985), pp. 122–85. For a somewhat earlier and very different feminist reading of sentimental novels like *Charlotte Temple*, see Wendy Martin, 'Profile: Susanna Rowson, Early American Novelist,' *Women's Studies* 2 (1974): 1–8; for a recent critique of Davidson's interpretation, see Klaus P. Hansen, 'The Sentimental Novel and Its Feminist Critique,' *Early American Literature*, 26 (1991): 39–54.

65. Medlicott, 'The Legend of Lucy Brewer,' 464.

66. *Female Marine*, p. 9.

at the end of the first installment: 'If what I have exposed to public view is sufficient to induce youths of my sex never to listen to the voice of love, unless sanctioned by paternal approbation, and to resist the impulse of inclination, when it runs counter to the precepts of religion and virtue, then, indeed, have I not written in vain.'[67] That moralistic warning was, in fact, taken nearly verbatim from Susanna Rowson's *Charlotte Temple*, the most popular American novel of the early republic.[68] Just like Lucy Brewer, Rowson warns her young female readers to 'listen not to the voice of love, unless sanctioned by paternal approbation' and to 'resist the impulse of inclination when it runs counter to the precepts of religion and virtue.'[69] At least one other extended passage from the *The Female Marine* is taken verbatim from *Charlotte Temple*; an attack on the sexual double standard in *The Awful Beacon* echoes Rowson's rhetoric of outrage; and there is other evidence of direct literary borrowing.[70]

The main obstacle to incorporating *The Female Marine* into the traditional canon of sentimental fiction is that Coverly's playful narrative flagrantly defies the main tenet of the formulaic seduction tale—that a sexual fall must be followed by anguished suffering and penitent death. Although Lucy does go through some hard times immediately following her seduction, she eventually turns her reversal to advantage, surviving three years of heroic military service and finally winning the hand of the wealthy Mr. West. Far from exhibiting the passive anguish of violated womanhood, Lucy demonstrates active courage, resourcefulness, and even good humor in the face of adversity.

The utter subversiveness of Lucy's story is accentuated by its

---

67. *Female Marine*, p. 51.
68. On the extraordinary popularity of *Charlotte Temple*, see Susanna Rowson, *Charlotte Temple: A Tale of Truth*, ed. Cathy N. Davidson (New York: Oxford University Press, 1986), pp. xi–xxxiii, passim.
69. Ibid., p. 29.
70. Compare passage in Rowson, *Charlotte Temple*, p. 32 to the nearly identical passage in *Female Marine*, pp. 22–23. Compare Rowson's rhetoric on pp. 28–29 to the attack on the sexual double standard in *The Awful Beacon*, pp. 45–46 (particularly the phrase 'Gracious heaven!' and the reference to men as 'monsters'). Also see discussion below on the lines of verse beneath frontispiece of *The Adventures of Louisa Baker*.

juxtaposition to one of the supplementary sketches appended to part three of the narrative. That brief sketch tells of Maria D\_\_\_\_, a sweet and pure, but naïve, young woman who innocently marries a 'weak, vicious and debauched man.' An unworthy husband, this man soon becomes a patron of Boston's vilest brothels, leading to poor Maria's passive decline and early death.[71] The sharp contrast between the fates of Lucy Brewer and Maria D\_\_\_\_ suggests that a bad marriage could be a greater disaster than an outright seduction. In the treacherous world of gender relations depicted by *The Female Marine*, a young woman's autonomy was ultimately more important than her virginity. Here was a message far more radical than that attributed by scholars like Cathy N. Davidson to conventional sentimental tales like *Charlotte Temple*.[72] Although it seems unlikely that Nathaniel Coverly (or Nathaniel Hill Wright) had women's liberation in mind when he set his literary pot to boiling, that message of female autonomy may help explain the narrative's appeal to the young ladies of early national Boston—and to enlightened academics today. Amid the sedate assemblage of Republican Wives, Republican Mothers, and True Women found in early national popular literature and in late twentieth-century scholarship, the female marine is indeed a welcome if unexpected intruder.[73]

III

As a resilient survivor of seduction, urban vice, and military combat, Lucy Brewer—and her aggressive approach to life—seem somehow distinctly modern. Fortunately, that casual observation can be tested against a rich if controversial body of theory and scholarship. The modernization model, formulated by social scientists during the 1960s, posits a fundamentally bipolar view of culture, society, and personality, built upon a contrast between the

---

71. *Female Marine*, pp. 135–41.
72. See Davidson, *Revolution and the Word*, pp. 83–150. On the other hand, a cynic might argue that Coverly's pamphlets are an elaborate ruse to convince the young women of New England to lower their guards on the unrealistic assumption that they would be able to recover as effectively as Lucy Brewer.
73. For scholarly discussions of those popular images, see works cited in note 2.

traditional and the modern. According to Richard D. Brown, the leading exponent of the theory as applied to early American history, traditional peoples tend to be fatalistic: 'The prevailing outlook of people in traditional society is one of acceptance or resignation toward life as it is. . . . There is neither the aspiration nor the expectation of spiritual or material improvement for society. . . . Innovation and novelty are viewed with suspicion.'[74] Brown describes the modern personality type as the polar opposite of the traditional; it is characterized by individual dynamism, autonomy, cosmopolitanism, flexibility, and a determination to master and manipulate the environment to advantage.[75]

There can be little doubt as to where 'Lucy Brewer' stands in reference to the divide between traditional and modern. The female marine violates traditional norms, exercises autonomy, travels widely, and demonstrates great flexibility in her determination to master her environment. She overcomes the stigma of her premarital seduction and defies conventional gender roles. More broadly, Coverly's pamphlets celebrate a society dominated by the modern impulse toward mastery. At one point in part three, Mr. West approvingly describes the reaction of Bostonians to a gale that had uprooted some large elms. Rather than respond fatalistically to an act of God or nature, the Bostonians simply take block and tackle and haul the trees back into place.[76] Just as the narrative celebrates the willful rise of a fallen woman, so also does it hail the resourceful raising of some fallen trees. In each case, the behavioral impulse is distinctly modern.

The modernity of *The Female Marine* is even more strikingly illustrated by Mr. West's patriotic disquisition at Plymouth Rock, an oration worthy of being quoted at some length:

> It was (continued he) scarcely 200 years ago [that the Pilgrims landed], and what was the now flourishing States of New England then! — an almost impenetrable forest, abounding with savages and beasts of prey!

74. Richard D. Brown, *Modernization: The Transformation of American Life 1600–1865* (New York: Hill and Wang, 1976), pp. 10–11.
75. Brown, *Modernization*, pp. 12–15.
76. *Female Marine*, p. 119.

... But with these dreary prospects the Pilgrims were not to be disheartened—they landed, and very soon changed the face of New England—they introduced symmetry by the assistance of all the instruments of art—the impenetrable woods were cleared, and made room for commodious habitations—the wild beasts were driven away and flocks of domestic animals supplied their place; whilst thorns and briars made way for rich harvests—the coasts were covered with towns, and the bays with ships—and thus the new world like the old became subject to man.[77]

A new world subject to man! It would be difficult to conceive of a vision of material progress and human mastery more remote from traditional Puritan piety with its insistence upon the covenanted community's humble dependence on a sovereign God.

Of course, modernization theory has its detractors, but even its most hostile critics have a hard time denying that a fundamental shift in American society and culture took place between the Revolution and the Civil War.[78] Those scholars have struggled to develop other ways of characterizing that transition, with many resorting to the concepts of republicanism and liberalism. Take, for example, Steven Watts's *The Republic Reborn*, which argues that the War of 1812 marked a key point of transition between social orders built on eighteenth-century republicanism and nineteenth-century liberalism. In contrast to modernization theorists who generally imply that modernization is a good thing, Watts suggests that the rise of liberalism was (in certain respects) a bad one, leading to psychological stress, deep anxieties, neurotic repression, fragmented personalities, and, finally, to the fratricidal bloodbath of the American Civil War.[79] Nathaniel Coverly's *The Female Marine*, it might be argued, conforms to the letter but not the spirit of Watts's thesis. While the War of 1812 did provide Lucy Brewer

77. *The Awful Beacon* (Boston: N. Coverly, Jr., 1816), pp. 22–23; for a somewhat shorter version of the same speech, see *Female Marine*, pp. 122–23.
78. For one prominent critic, see James A. Henretta, '"Modernization": Toward a False Synthesis,' *Reviews in American History* 5 (September 1977): 445–52.
79. See Steven Watts, *The Republic Reborn: War and the Making of Liberal America, 1790–1820* (Baltimore: Johns Hopkins University Press, 1987), pp. 166–72, 271–73, 320–21, and passim. My discussion here obviously oversimplifies Watts's complex and provocative argument.

Fig. 2. An unusual depiction of Lucy West (née Brewer) as a bourgeois matron. Frontispiece of *The Awful Beacon* (Boston: N. Coverly, Jun., 1816). Courtesy, American Antiquarian Society. For more typical images of the female marine, see Appendix B.

with her entrée into a world of bourgeois liberalism, that outcome did not lead to stress, anxiety, and repression but to personal autonomy, restored self-confidence, and a happy marriage.[80]

Still, Watts's argument is useful here in reminding us that *The Female Marine* is not simply a generic embodiment of the modern worldview but rather a reflection of cultural attitudes in a particular time and place. That is, it reflects the period of national unity, optimism, and patriotism that followed the Battle of New Orleans in 1815 and climaxed during the early years of the Monroe administration in the so-called Era of Good Feelings—a happy interlude that was abruptly terminated by the financial and sectional crises of 1819. In recent years the very concept of an Era of Good Feelings has fallen into some disrepute, even among textbook writers. In *The American Pageant*, for example, Bailey and Kennedy claim that the label is 'something of a misnomer.'[81] One prominent scholar has recently gone so far as to dub the period the 'Era of *Bad* Feelings.'[82] Yet I would argue that an Era of Good Feelings did, in fact, occur—at least in New England—and would offer *The Female Marine* as proof.

While it is on one level a cautionary tale of seduction, *The Female Marine* is on another a good-humored and optimistic celebration of the patriotic valor of an American woman. In fact, Coverly's changing frontispieces for the pamphlets neatly suggest that the patriotic component of their appeal became increasingly important over time. (See Appendix B.) The original frontispiece of part one consists of an upper-torso portrait of the heroine in a low-cut dress that accentuates her breasts; the text beneath the portrait includes a few lines of sentimental verse referring to her seduction—lifted from the title page of *Charlotte Temple*.[83] The frontispiece to an edition of part two contains the same portrait

---

80. As will become clear by the end of this essay, I believe that *The Female Marine* reflected a good deal of social anxiety and psychic stress, placing it more in line with Watts's interpretation than this paragraph might suggest.
81. See Bailey and Kennedy, *American Pageant*, I: 228.
82. Sean Wilentz, *Major Problems in the Early Republic, 1787–1848* (Lexington, Mass.: D. C. Heath, 1992), p. 333, emphasis added.
83. *The Adventures of Louisa Baker*, frontispiece; Rowson, *Charlotte Temple*, p. 17.

but with a military hat crudely added to the figure, the bust more modestly concealed, and the seduction verses removed.[84] The frontispieces of composite editions of *The Female Marine* generally portray a somewhat androgynous woman standing at attention with a musket in her hand and a frigate in the background. A vignette of the great seal of the United States appears on the front wrapper of one of those editions.[85] (See Fig. 1.) Finally, the frontispiece of the 1818 edition—the last known—depicts a woman in military dress waving an American flag.[86] Over the course of its publishing history, then, the iconography of the narrative seems to have shifted in emphasis from sentimental seduction to patriotic adventure. In the Era of Good Feelings, even a fallen woman could feel good about herself—and about her country!

To recapitulate, the War of 1812 ended in 1815, the year in which the first two parts of Lucy Brewer's narrative were published. At least nineteen printings or editions of the various parts of the narrative were issued, mostly in Boston, during the years 1815 through 1818. The Era of Good Feelings is conventionally considered to have ended the following year—in 1819. Significantly, the actual phrase 'Era of Good Feelings' originated in Boston. It was coined in the summer of 1817 in response to the warm reception given by the city's inhabitants to the newly elected President of the United States, the Virginian James Monroe, during a good will tour of formerly hostile New England.[87] The greeting was in many respects reminiscent of that given to Old Ironsides two years earlier, complete with musical band, ringing bells, waving flags, and countless citizens turned out in the streets.[88] It is certainly tempting to speculate that at least some among the throngs that warmly greeted the chief of state owned well-thumbed copies of *The Female Marine*.

84. *The Adventures of Lucy Brewer* (Boston: H. Trumbull, 1815), frontispiece.
85. *The Female Marine* ([Boston?]: [N. Coverly, Jr.?], June 19, 1816), front cover and frontispiece.
86. *The Female Marine* ([Boston?]: Printed for the Author [by N. Coverly, Jr.?], 1818), frontispiece.
87. John M. Blum et al., *The National Experience: A History of the United States*, 5th ed. (New York: Harcourt Brace Jovanovich, 1981), p. 196.
88. See *The Yankee*, July 4, 1817, p. 3.

Yet beneath the exuberant good feelings of Boston's citizens may have lurked anxiety, ambivalence, and even guilt. Those darker feelings can also help explain why so many readers embraced *The Female Marine*. In her recent study of 'cross-dressing and cultural anxiety,' literary critic Marjorie Garber argues that 'one of the most consistent and effective functions of the transvestite in culture is to indicate the place of what I call "category crisis," disrupting and calling attention to cultural, social, or aesthetic dissonances.' According to Garber, then, the appearance of cross-dressing as a cultural motif typically suggests the presence within the culture of some other source of 'crisis' or 'dissonance,' not always directly related to issues of gender and sexuality.[89]

One social crisis or dissonance reflected in *The Female Marine* was an increasing anxiety among Bostonians of various social classes concerning the perceived growth of urban vice and disorder during the first decades of the nineteenth century. Between 1790 and 1825, Boston was transformed from a relatively cohesive town of 18,000 inhabitants to a heterogeneous metropolis containing more than three times as many people. As growing population density and fluidity increased the anonymity of city life, traditional social controls weakened and even long-standing social vices assumed new and more threatening forms. At the same time, pious evangelicals (inspired by the Second Great Awakening) and civic-minded business leaders were becoming less and less tolerant of commercialized sex and other perceived manifestations of urban depravity and disorder. That was the context, historian Barbara Hobson explains, in which Bostonians of the 1810s and 1820s first 'discovered' prostitution as a serious social problem.[90]

Indeed, it was at precisely the period when Coverly was marketing his female-marine pamphlets that Boston residents of differing social ranks first mobilized to combat prostitution. Working-class truckmen seem to have rioted on Negro Hill in 1816 in an effort

---

89. See Marjorie Garber, *Vested Interests: Cross-Dressing & Cultural Anxiety* (New York: Routledge, 1992), pp. 9–17, quoted on p. 16.
90. See Hobson, *Uneasy Virtue*, pp. 12–14, quoted.

to destroy the homes of black residents whom they perceived to be linked to 'bad' women.[91] Also in that year, middle-class social reformers began to establish a series of new organizations and institutions to combat sexual vice. And several years later, Mayor Josiah Quincy of Boston personally spearheaded urban America's first sustained police crackdown on prostitution.[92] *The Female Marine's* image of a cross-dressing prostitute-turned-patriot both reflected the new anxiety over problems of urban vice and embodied a wishful fantasy of their resolution through individual exertion and moral reform. One cannot help but wonder whether any of Boston's prostitutes—reportedly prominent among Coverly's regular customers—were inspired by the story to mend their ways.[93]

A second, perhaps even more acute, source of anxiety embedded in Coverly's pamphlets related to the just-concluded War of 1812. To use Garber's terms, the people of New England, particularly of Federalist port towns like Boston, must have felt an extreme identity crisis stemming from the ideological dissonance between their region's notorious disloyalty throughout the military struggle with England and their new-found patriotism at the conclusion of the war. As Bailey and Kennedy explain: 'In a sense America fought two enemies simultaneously: old England and New Eng-

---

91. See *Dreadful Riot on Negro Hill!* ([Boston?: 1816?), broadside. A copy of that rare broadside, now in the collections of the Library Company of Philadelphia, is described in Catalogue 57, M & S Rare Books, Inc., Providence, R. I., 1993. I am grateful to Daniel G. Siegel of M & S Rare Books and James N. Green of the Library Company of Philadelphia for photocopies of that broadside. It should be noted that anti-brothel riots did occasionally occur in Boston and other cities during the colonial period; see Carl Bridenbaugh, *Cities in the Wilderness: The First Century of Urban Life in America, 1625–1742* (1938; reprint, New York: Oxford University Press, 1971), pp. 388–89; Bridenbaugh, *Cities in Revolt: Urban Life in America, 1743–1776* (1955; reprint, New York: Oxford University Press, 1971), pp. 316–17.

92. See Hobson, *Uneasy Virtue*, pp. 11–23; also see David J. Pivar, *Purity Crusade: Sexual Morality and Social Control, 1868–1900* (Westport, Conn.: Greenwood Publishing Corp., 1973), pp. 23–24. Among the organizations and institutions established were the Boston Society for the Moral and Religious Instruction of the Poor, the Female Missionary Society, and the Penitent Females' Refuge.

93. For the suggestion that prostitutes figured prominently among Coverly's regular customers, see the reference to "the Ann street population" in Unidentified Newspaper Clipping.

land. New England gold holders probably lent more dollars to the British than to the federal treasury. New England farmers sent huge quantities of supplies and foodstuffs to Canada, enabling British armies to invade New York. New England governors stubbornly refused to permit their militia to serve outside their own states.'[94]

Put simply, for three years, many leading New Englanders had been traitors; but by the spring and summer of 1815, the people of that region desperately wanted to believe that they were patriots. The situation must have been particularly poignant for such working-class Bostonians as the sailors who eagerly purchased Coverly's naval broadsides. Many such men undoubtedly supported the war effort, and voted Republican, through the darkest days of the conflict. Yet they may have nonetheless felt implicated—and, as employees of Federalist merchants, may have been practically implicated—in their region's notorious disloyalty. How then did Boston patriots, whether newborn or long-frustrated, resolve their ideological dissonance or identity crisis? Can there be any doubt? They rushed out and purged their collective guilt and anxiety by snapping up copies of *The Female Marine*.[95]

For whether or not Nathaniel Coverly, Jr., or his hack writer, or their readers fully understood it, *The Female Marine* is a brilliant allegory for the ideological inconstancy of mercantile New England between 1812 and 1815, an allegory in which the binary categories of male and female—of sexual virtue and sexual vice—represent the polar opposites of patriotism and disloyalty. Just as Lucy Brewer is seduced and prostituted by corrupt companions and commercialized sex, so was New England seduced and prosti-

94. Bailey and Kennedy, *American Pageant*, I: 213.
95. Recall that Coverly advertised his pamphlets in *Republican* newspapers. On the purchase of Coverly's broadsides by Boston sailors, see Unidentified Newspaper Clipping. On the probability that sailors tended to vote Republican, see James M. Banner, Jr., *To the Hartford Convention* (New York: Alfred A. Knopf, 1970), pp. 172, note, and 193–94. However, it should be remembered that a large majority of Boston men voted Federalist throughout the War of 1812 and even in its aftermath; see note 3. Obviously, ambivalent or aroused patriotism—whether on the part of Federalists or Republicans—would not have motivated *all* purchasers of *The Female Marine*; others were undoubtedly drawn by prurient, sentimental, or romantic interest, or by the appeal of female adventure.

tuted by the lure of British commerce. Just as Lucy Brewer successfully reverses her fall by changing sex and joining the crew of the frigate *Constitution*, so did New England symbolically annul her treachery by exuberantly embracing the Constitution—embodied both by the actual ship of that name and by the founding father James Monroe. Just as Lucy Brewer affirms her miraculously restored virtue by marrying Mr. West—and that name is a tip-off to the allegory—so did New England, during the Era of Good Feelings, seek to renew her political covenant with the rest of the United States, and especially with the frontier regions (a.k.a. the West) that had supported the war all along. In short, *The Female Marine* served to reassure anxious New Englanders that past errors could be corrected and forgiven, that a happy marriage could follow an unhappy seduction, and that New Englanders could feel proud of themselves both as loyal daughters of the Pilgrims and as brave sons of Columbia. It would be hard to imagine a more suitable fantasy for an Era of Good Feelings.

## APPENDIX A

### Editions of *The Female Marine* and Component Parts

This list is based upon American Antiquarian Society holdings; Ralph R. Shaw and Richard H. Shoemaker, comp., *American Bibliography* (New York: Scarecrow Press, 1963); and the *National Union Catalogue*.

### 1815

*The Adventures of Louisa Baker* (New-York: Luther Wales, [August? 1815]). Shaw and Shoemaker 33907 and 36517.

*An Affecting Narrative of Louisa Baker* (New York: Luther Wales; reprint, Boston: Nathaniel Coverly, Jun., 1815). Shaw and Shoemaker 33907 and 36518.

*An Affecting Narrative of Louisa Baker*, 2nd ed. (New York: Luther Wales; reprint, Boston: Nathaniel Coverly, Jun., [September?] 1815). Shaw and Shoemaker 36519.

*The Adventures of Lucy Brewer* (Boston: N. Coverly, Jr., [November?] 1815). Shaw and Shoemaker 33794 and 36516.

*The Adventures of Lucy Brewer* (Boston: H. Trumbull, 1815). Shaw and Shoemaker 36515.

### 1816

*The Female Marine* ([Boston?]: [N. Coverly, Jr.?], January 1, 1816). Shaw and Shoemaker 39743.

*The Awful Beacon* (Boston: N. Coverly, Jr., [May?] 1816). Shaw and Shoemaker 37081, 39742, and 39784.

*The Female Marine* ([Boston?]: [N. Coverly, Jr.?], May 30, 1816). Shaw and Shoemaker 39744.

*The Female Marine* ([Boston?]: [N. Coverly, Jr.?], June 19, 1816). Shaw and Shoemaker 37745.

*The Female Marine*, 2nd ed. ([Boston?]:[N. Coverly, Jr.?], June 24, 1816). Shaw and Shoemaker 39746 and 39785.

*An Affecting Narrative of Louisa Baker* (Boston: Nathaniel Coverly; reprint, New York: John Low, 1816). AAS, not in Shaw and Shoemaker.

*An Affecting Narrative of Louisa Baker* (New York: 1816). Not in AAS or Shaw and Shoemaker; NUC only.

*An Affecting Narrative of Louisa Baker* (Portsmouth, N.H.: Printed for the Purchaser, 1816). Shaw and Shoemaker 36687.

## The Female Marine

*The Adventures of Lucy Brewer* (Boston: N. Coverly, Jun., 1816). Shaw and Shoemaker 37080 and 39783.

*The Female Marine* ([Boston?]: Printed for the Publisher [N. Coverly, Jr.?], [ca. 1816]). Shaw and Shoemaker 39748.

*The Female Marine* (Hartwick, [N.Y.]: L. & B. Todd, [ca. 1816]). AAS, not in Shaw and Shoemaker.

*The Female Marine*, 10th ed. ([Boston?]: Printed for the Proprietor [N. Coverly, Jr.?], 1816). Shaw and Shoemaker 39747.

### 1817

*The Female Marine*, 5th ed. (Boston: Printed for the Purchaser [by N. Coverly, Jr.?], 1817). Shaw and Shoemaker 40315 and 42851.

### 1818

*The Female Marine*, 4th ed. ([Boston]: Printed for the Author [by N. Coverly, Jr.?], 1818). Shaw and Shoemaker 46735.

## APPENDIX B

### Iconography of the Female Marine

A. Frontispiece of *The Adventures of Louisa Baker* (New York: Luther Wales, [1815]). This is the earliest known image of the female marine. Courtesy, American Antiquarian Society.

B. Frontispiece of *The Adventures of Lucy Brewer* (Boston: H. Trumbull, 1815). Note that this is essentially the same portrait as in the Wales pamphlet, but with a military hat crudely added to the figure, the bust more modestly concealed, the subject's name changed, and the seduction verses replaced by an advertisement. Courtesy, American Antiquarian Society.

C. Frontispiece of *The Female Marine* ([Boston?]:[N. Coverly, Jr.?], June 19, 1816). Courtesy, American Antiquarian Society.

D. Frontispiece of *The Female Marine* ([Boston?]: Printed for the Author [N. Coverly, Jr.?], 1818). This is the last known nineteenth-century edition of *The Female Marine*. Courtesy, American Antiquarian Society.

Frontispiece of *The Adventures of Louisa Baker* (New York: Luther Wales, [1815]). Courtesy, American Antiquarian Society.

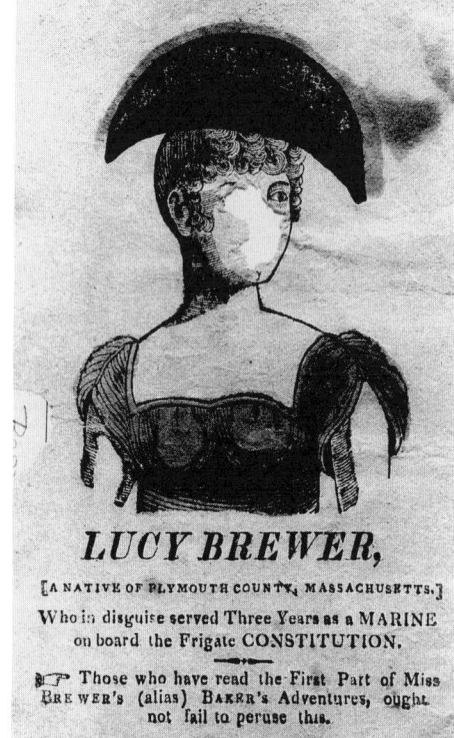

Frontispiece of *The Adventures of Lucy Brewer* (Boston: H. Trumbull, 1815). Courtesy, American Antiquarian Society.

## Erratum

The captions for the illustrations on page 393 of the *Proceedings of the American Antiquarian Society* (103, part 2) were inadvertently misplaced. The frontispiece of the 1816 edition of *The Female Marine* is the woman standing at attention with a musket in her hand; the frontispiece of the 1818 edition is the woman in military dress waving an American flag.

Frontispiece of *The Female Marine* ([Boston?]: [N. Coverly, Jr.?], June 19, 1816). Courtesy, American Antiquarian Society.

Frontispiece of *The Female Marine* ([Boston?]: Printed for the Author [N. Coverly, Jr.?], 1818). Courtesy, American Antiquarian Society.